EP

On Thanksgiving Day

El Día de Acción de Gracias

written by Judy Zocchi

illustrated by Rebecca Wallis

dingles & company New Jersey

First printing

PUBLISHED BY dingles&company
P.O. Box 508 · Sea Girt, New Jersey · 08750
WEBSITE: www.dingles.com · E-MAIL: info@dingles.com

Library of Congress Catalog Card No.: 2004092707
ISBN: 1-891997-75-0

Printed in the United States of America

For Dad, who understood the true spirit of Thanksgiving.

ART DIRECTION & DESIGN Barbie Lambert
PHOTOGRAPHY Sara Sagliano
ENGLISH EDITED BY Andrea Curley
SPANISH EDITED BY John Page
RESEARCH AND ADDITIONAL COPY WRITTEN BY Robert Neal Kanner
EDUCATIONAL CONSULTANTS Kathleen Miller & Anita Tarquinio-Marcocci
DESIGN ASSISTANT Erin Collity
PRE-PRESS BY Pixel Graphics

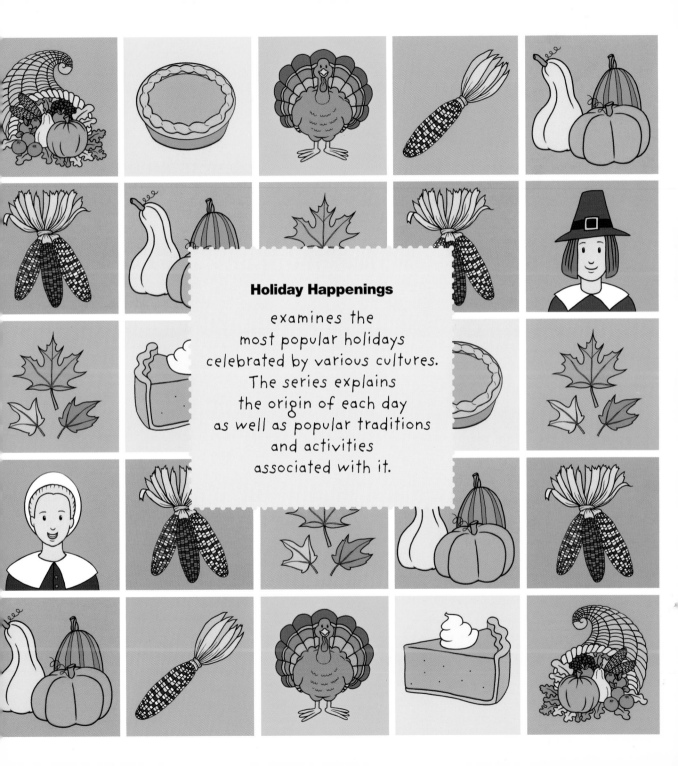

Holiday Happenings

examines the
most popular holidays
celebrated by various cultures.
The series explains
the origin of each day
as well as popular traditions
and activities
associated with it.

On Thanksgiving Day you might help bake a turkey

El Día de Acción de Gracias puedes ayudar a cocinar un pavo

and make mashed potatoes with chives.

y hacer puré de papas con cebollana.

Then you set the table before
the company arrives.

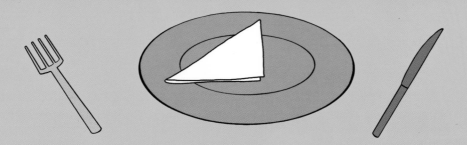

Luego puedes poner la mesa
antes que la visita llegue.

On Thanksgiving Day you could go to a football game

El Día de Acción de Gracias puedes ir a un partido de fútbol americano

Thanksgiving Day brings together families and friends. Sometimes people travel from great distances to be together on this day of thanksgiving.

with your family and friends.

con tu familia y amigos.

El Día de Acción de Gracias trae juntos a las familias y a los amigos. Algunas veces la gente viaja de grandes distancias para estar junta en este día de acción de gracias.

If you cheer too much, you'll lose your voice before the game ends!

Si animas mucho con gritos, ¡perderás tu voz antes que termine el partido!

On Thanksgiving Day you might put on a play about Pilgrims

El Día de Acción de Gracias puedes presentar un drama de los Peregrinos

and Indians, and how they
made peace.

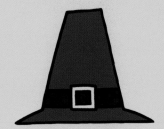

y los Indios Americanos, y cómo
hicieron la paz.

In the last scene you'll show
the first Thanksgiving feast!

¡En la última escena presentarás
el primer banquete
del Día de Acción de Gracias!

On Thanksgiving Day you'll all hold hands

El Día de Acción de Gracias todos se tomarán de las manos

and give thanks before you eat.

y darán gracias antes de comer.

After dinner you'll bring out
pumpkin pie for a treat!

¡Después de la cena sacarán el
pastel de calabaza para el postre!

The first Thanksgiving Day was celebrated in 1621 in Plymouth, Massachusetts. It was a three-day feast made by the English settlers, called Pilgrims, and the Native Americans who lived in the area. The Pilgrims had come to America the year before on a ship called the Mayflower. At first the Pilgrims and the natives had fought over the land, but now they were at peace. The Pilgrims wanted to celebrate their first good harvest. They also wanted to honor their new friendship with the native people and their new lives in America. Together, the Pilgrims and the natives hunted wild turkey, other fowl, and deer and gathered vegetables for the feast. Today, Thanksgiving is celebrated across the United States on the fourth Thursday of November as a way of giving thanks for everything good.

El primer Día de Acción de Gracias se celebró en 1621 en Plymouth, Massachussets. Fue un banquete de tres días hecho por los colonos ingleses, llamados Peregrinos, y los Indios Americanos que vivían en el área. Los Peregrinos habían venido a América el año antes en una nave llamada el Mayflower. Al principio los Peregrinos y los indígenas habían peleado por la tierra, pero ahora estaban en paz. Los Peregrinos querían celebrar su primera cosecha buena. También querían honrar su amistad nueva con la gente indígena y sus vidas nuevas en América. Juntos, los Peregrinos y los indígenas cazaron pavo salvaje, otras aves y ciervo, y recogieron la cosecha para el banquete. Ahora, el Día de Acción de Gracias se celebra a través los Estados Unidos el cuarto jueves de noviembre como modo de dar acción de gracias por todo bueno.

DID YOU KNOW...

Use the Holiday Happenings series to expose children to the world around them.

- On Thanksgiving eve, it is traditional for the president of the United States to pardon a turkey from being cooked and send it back to the farm! This custom started more than 50 years ago with Harry S Truman.
- According to one poultry expert, the heaviest turkey ever raised weighed 86 pounds, about the size of a large golden retriever, and was raised in England.
- The Pilgrims didn't use forks; they ate with their fingers, spoons, and knives. They also used the same cloth napkin to pick up hot food and wipe their hands.
- Only male turkeys (toms) gobble. Females (hens) make a type of clicking noise.

BUILDING CHARACTER...

Use the Holiday Happenings series to help instill positive character traits in your children. This Thanksgiving emphasize Gratitude.

- What are you thankful for?
- How can you show someone that you are thankful?
- What were the Pilgrims thankful for?
- What should we be thankful to the Pilgrims for?

CULTURE CONNECTION...

Use the Holiday Happenings series to expand children's view of other cultures.

- Find out which countries have a holiday similar to Thanksgiving.
- How do they celebrate their holiday?
- Are these celebrations similar to the way you celebrate Thanksgiving?

TRY SOMETHING NEW...

Give your parents or grandparents a handmade–not store-bought–thank-you card to thank them for all they do for you.

For more information on the Holiday Happenings series or to find activities that coordinate with it, explore our website at **www.dingles.com**.

Craft

Grateful Turkey Talk

Goal: To make a Thanksgiving centerpiece that encourages family and friends to express how grateful they are for one another.

Materials: small brown paper bag, newspaper, stapler, colored construction paper (brown or tan, orange, red, and yellow), crayons, scissors, glue, small pieces of writing paper and pencil; items found in nature, such as sticks, leaves, pinecones, acorns, etc.

Directions:

1. Gather materials.
2. Stuff a brown paper bag with newspaper until it is full. Staple it closed.
3. Trace 2 hands on the brown or tan construction paper and cut them out.
4. On the thumb part of each handprint, draw 2 small eyes, a triangular beak, and a gobbler (wattle) with the crayons. Glue 1 turkey handprint on each side of the paper bag with the eyes facing out.
5. Draw 4 turkey feet on the orange construction paper and cut them out. Then glue the feet to the bottom of the bag under the decorated turkey handprints.
6. Place a piece of construction paper in the center of the table. Put the turkey centerpiece on top.
7. With an adult, go outside and gather some objects from nature.
8. Place the objects around the turkey centerpiece.
9. Cut the writing paper into pieces and give one to each person at the table. Have each person write something that he or she is grateful for on it.
10. Place the pieces of paper around the turkey centerpiece.
11. Read what each person has written. Ask your family and friends to discuss each expression of gratitude.
12. Imagine! You just started a "Grateful Turkey Talk" on Thanksgiving Day.

Judy Zocchi

is the author of the Global Adventures, Holiday Happenings, Click & Squeak's Computer Basics, and Paulie and Sasha series. She is a writer and lyricist who holds a bachelor's degree in fine arts/theater from Mount Saint Mary's College and a master's degree in educational theater from New York University. She lives in Manasquan, New Jersey, with her husband, David.

Rebecca Wallis

was born in Cornwall, England, and has a bachelor's degree in illustration from Falmouth College of Arts. She has illustrated a wide variety of books for children, and she divides her time between Cornwall and London.